EXPECTATIONS

A TRUE ADOPTION STORY

TONY BERTAUSKI

PREFACE

I write fiction. I make up stories.

This is not one of them.

This story is true. Some minor details have been altered and names changed, but the story itself is true. At some point, you won't believe it. Hell, I don't believe some of it and I was there. It's a story about crises. It's about resolution, about life prevailing.

It's about adoption.

This is not a step-by-step guide on how to turn lemons into lemonade. I'm not an expert in crisis management or adoption. There was plenty of the luck to make all of this happen. This is just one story.

It happens to be true.

ONE

This story starts with a girl named Heather.

She was a fair-skinned redhead who was a year behind me in middle school. We had never said a word to each other. We didn't run with the same crowds. I had no idea if she noticed me, but I noticed her. Middle school was all about hormones. She was cute. Attractive.

Of course I noticed.

She got straight As and didn't cuss. She didn't stay out late on weekends, played saxophone in the band, and cheered on the sidelines with pom-poms with more school spirit than the mascot.

She was preppy and wore what was in style. This was the early eighties—double Polo shirts, leg warmers, and acid-washed denim. She wasn't an easy girl. No one got past first base with her, as far as I knew.

She was a good girl.

I wasn't exactly a bad boy, but my crowd wasn't preppy. I played football, dipped Skoal, stole from my parents' wallets and lived in arcades. I wasn't a stellar student, but I wasn't the worst. My run with girls was about the same.

Not the best, not the worst.

Michelle was my high school girlfriend. We did what most high school kids did, and we were doing it with her mom in the next room. It was exciting and daring and stupid. We were back and forth for about a year or so.

At some point during that time, there was Heather.

Every Sunday, I saw her in church and watched her approach communion. That was the only thing I liked about mass, waiting to see her come back. I would imagine what it was like to date a girl like that. We didn't seem to be a match, but somehow it happened.

For two weeks.

There were no fireworks during that time. Maybe we held hands, I don't remember. After two glorious weeks of tepid affection, she broke it off. She was good about it, telling me face-to-face. I pretended like it was no big deal and probably called Michelle the next day.

While she was a senior, I moved on to college. Occasionally, I would see her at a party when I came home, but we never talked. I saw her at church, but we were still in very different social circles.

Everything changed the following summer.

She broke up with her high school boyfriend and told her sister, who told my buddy, who told me that she was interested. I told him to tell her sister to tell her I was too.

That's how it started.

OUR FIRST DATE was to the state fair. She came to my house dressed in red and white. As it happened, I was too. That night we made out on her mom's couch until our lips were numb. The next morning, I showed up at her summer job unannounced. She lit up and I did too. "I can definitely say," I said, "I'm in lust with you."

We did the same thing the next night.

She was eighteen years old and I was nineteen. We were at the beginning of a long relationship. It didn't take long before the road got bumpy. They were the best of times with a lot of crying in between. We broke up, got back together, broke up, she moved, I stayed, she traveled, I wrote letters, she sent pictures.

It was reality TV without an audience.

Heather finished one year of college when she and a friend lived in Florida. They did food and bev and saved enough money to travel to Australia. After a few years of world experience, she returned to the Midwest.

She attended Southern Illinois University in Carbondale. I was still there. We both expected to get back together and then it didn't happen. It was more me than her. I was having a hard time with commitment. I didn't know why because I had nothing else going on. School was almost over and I was clueless.

She was upset.

Of course she was. I had written all these letters while she was travelling and then I was like, meh. What a dick. It was heartbreaking, but she stayed in Carbondale and got her groove back. Life went on.

She was living in an apartment on the other side of

town with roommates and parties and the whole college experience. And without me.

It was the fall of 1989.

Having declared a major late, I stayed an extra semester to finish undergrad. I was still living in a house ravaged by years of partying. We had trashed a slumlord's house while passing classes, living on our own and doing whatever we wanted. Some of my roommates had already graduated and moved on. Real life was waiting for me. It was time to grow up, become an adult, get a job, pay some bills and live happily ever after. My roommates seemed ready for that.

It wasn't working out for me.

I was majoring in plant and soil science because I worked on a golf course in high school. No one in my family knew a thing about plants and I was going to be a grower. It was lonely and frightening and I wasn't ready.

Heather and I were occasionally talking. She was getting on just fine without me. I spent Saturday nights in front of the television, eating ramen noodles and changing channels. I'd call her, sometimes hearing a party in the background. Sometimes she'd come over and spend the night.

We had become friends with benefits.

She was hopeful it would be more than that, but not really invested in it. She'd finally made a healthy break from me with no expectations. I had no idea what I was doing. Life was speeding and I was white-knuckle frightened. There were nights she would stay over and I didn't want her to leave, but didn't know how to say it. What happened if I lost interest again?

What the hell is wrong with me?

October 1989, we took a road trip to Eastern Illinois University to spend the weekend with her sister and my buddy, the same couple that hooked us up almost four years earlier. We were lying in a pile of blankets on a Sunday morning, lazy and content.

Things seemed good.

We were heading in the right direction. I was hopeful that it would work this time. I really liked her. I loved her. I just didn't know how to love. I wanted to. Why was it so hard?

The story starts here.

I WAS SLEEPING on the floor on a makeshift bed of blankets one night. It was the middle of the week, classes were the next morning. It was still dark when my bedroom door swung open. The knob hit the wall and I shot up. The dim light of an alarm clock illuminated someone in my doorway. She lunged at me.

Heather.

She was hysterical—a sweaty, tear-soaked, snotty mess. I couldn't make out a word. All I could do was hold her. It was really late and she had come all the way across town. Words gushed from her, one syllable overlapping the next and nothing making sense. Something really bad had happened. And then a word rose out of the puddle.

Pregnant.

Yeah. She was twenty-one years old and still in college. This was not part of her plan. Mine, either.

This also wasn't why she was so upset.

TWO

We've all had those moments.

The one where you miss that last step, the panic rises. For a second, you're not sure you'll ever hit the ground. You just keep falling because this can't happen to me. It's surreal, overwhelming. It's all of that packed into the red pill and then down the hatch.

Reality.

I was twenty-two years old. I was still in college, sleeping on the floor, staying up too late and wondering where I might work that summer. I was still a kid. We both were. And we were huddled in the corner of a craphole house, the night shattered by her sobbing.

My roommates didn't say a thing. Not then or in the morning. Midnight arguments were not the norm, but they weren't that unusual, either. They probably heard the door open, heard the wailing and went right back to sleep. The bedroom walls were basically paneling, but they couldn't understand what she was saying. She was crying on my chest and I couldn't understand.

Except that one word.

SO NOW WHAT?

This was not in the plan. I wasn't sure I could take care of myself. I was heading into depression. I had been for quite some time, just didn't have it labeled yet. I was frightened, confused, and aimless. School was about done and I had no idea what I wanted to do or why. Like many kids that age, the transition to adulthood was long and winding and I was thoroughly lost.

So I lay in the blankets, holding her. Whatever my issues were at the moment, they would take a backseat. It forced me to set them aside, stop focusing on myself and be there for her. In a way, it was a relief. I wasn't thinking of me. I had a job to do.

Grow up.

The storm eventually passed. Her sobbing settled. She was able to breathe without hitching. And then she told me. She had taken a pregnancy test because she was late and it turned out the price was right. But that wasn't the showstopper. That wasn't the reason she drove across town in the middle of the night or the reason she was inconsolable.

I don't know if you're the father.

Bit of a left turn there I didn't see coming.

We weren't an exclusive couple. We weren't really a couple. I was still eating ramen noodles on Saturday nights and she was living her life. She had been with someone that month. It wasn't easy for me to hear, but it was harder for her to say. She was a good girl.

This wasn't supposed to happen.

This was a detour. And on this detour was a fork in the road. I was on one side and a guy named Steve was on the other. In the meantime, we had a big red pill to swallow.

After the words left her, the storm returned with all the guilt and shame and sorrow that one would expect. It was out there; she'd said it. It was real now. I wasn't angry, not even hurt. Maybe it was the depression that kept me from heading down those paths, or that there was this person I loved in genuine, utter distress. Despite my feelings about it, I needed not to go that way. I could (and would) feel all the hurt and sorrow for myself at a later time, a tidy little mess I would eventually address many years later.

For now, there was this.

So we lay there on a pile of blankets. In the morning we'd figure out what to do. Two kids, barely in their twenties, with a baby eight months away.

Time to grow up.

THREE

There was some upside to our situation.

First off, we had eight *months*, not eight *minutes*, to figure this out. There was time to breathe, time to think.

Secondly, we were alone.

We were still kids, but not exactly. We didn't live with our parents or even near them. My roommates didn't say anything. They'd either slept through the home invasion or chalked it up as an argument. This was the space we needed to let the pieces settle before sorting them out.

In the meantime, life continued.

We still had classes to attend, exams to take. Bills to pay.

We confirmed the pregnancy with a doctor. That was a jab that followed the hook. There was a sliver of hope the test she took was wrong. It wasn't. We did the checkups and brought home the prenatals and no one knew about it. Just us.

What are the options?

First there was parenting. I was struggling with my own life. It was going to take years to figure my own shit out. I had no idea how deep that mess was going to be, but I knew it would take some time. Throw a newborn on top of that and all three of us were going down.

Heather wasn't ready, either. She was twenty-one years old. She was more emotionally fit than I was, but she was still a kid. Besides, our relationship was anything but stable. It had a chance but needed time.

It wasn't ready for a baby.

There was also the issue of the third party. I might not be the father. That was a bit of a wrinkle. Steve didn't know about this yet. We would eventually cross that bridge. Right now, we had to answer a question.

Could we raise a child?

If we had to, we could feed him and clothe him, send him to school, sure. But getting married, staying married, being happy... all of that looked choppy. We could be parents, but not the parents we wanted to be. We needed to figure out our own lives first. After that, get our relationship working. If we got to that point, we would have something to share with a child. It was clear we weren't there yet.

So parenting was out.

That led us to the next option: abortion. We were prochoice. We believed in and supported a woman's right to choose to end an unwanted pregnancy.

We chose not to.

The answer came easy for both of us and, in that regard, we were lucky. We seemed to fall in step with our decisions, both landing on the same squares as we went along. Abortion was out, case closed.

I don't know why we felt so sure about that, but I think it was for the same reason we didn't want to parent. We loved this child. It's weird to say, he didn't have a heartbeat at that point, and we already wanted the best for him. Parenting wasn't it, and neither was abortion.

Now what?

We had friends who had been adopted in the late sixties. They didn't know their birth parents and neither did their adoptive parents. All transactions were made through a third party. That was how things worked. A birth mother placed her child with an agency and the agency placed the child with an adoptive family. Nobody knew anybody and life went on.

We weren't sure we could do that.

One thing had become clear, a factor that was guiding all our decisions. The health and well-being of this child was first and foremost. He was top priority. What was best for him? It was why we couldn't parent, why we couldn't abort. And it was why we couldn't drop him off at an adoption agency and hope for the best. We were out of options.

Until we met with an adoption caseworker.

FOUR

Heather and I grew up Catholic.

We still remember the hard pews and the long Sunday mornings, the monotone sermons and dry wafers that clung to the roof of our mouths. We weren't Catholic anymore, but Catholic Social Services (CSS) was one of the adoption agencies in the area. There were also attorneys who specialized in adoption, but CSS offered counselling services in addition to developing an open adoption plan where we could pick the parents.

We liked that idea.

The social worker met us in a drab room with wood paneling and Berber carpeting. It smelled churchy. We wanted to know about open adoption. What was it? How did it work? Could we pick the parents? Could we stay in touch after the adoption?

The social worker was mildly shocked.

Maybe it was the way I was dressed or that we were so excited. Open adoption wasn't that common and we were on the edge of our seat because this was it. We knew it; we could feel it.

This was what we wanted.

The social worker explained that adoptive couples put together profiles. These were mostly narratives that told us a little bit about themselves, their background, education, philosophies, etc. If we liked someone, she told us, we could meet them if they were agreeable. There was no pressure to say yes, no pressure to follow through. In fact, we could change our minds at the very last minute.

This is it.

We were locked in. We weren't changing our minds. We couldn't be good parents, but we could *find* good parents. We were going into this wide-eyed and awake.

Heather told Steve the situation.

She was pregnant and there was a chance that he could be the father. She had made a decision to make an adoption plan, and he could be involved if he wanted. If not, we had it covered. He could attend to the legalizing if he was the parent. He was fine with that.

That made things easier.

We returned home for Christmas break and told our parents. Initially, we didn't mention Steve. The news was best served as simply as possible. Heather was pregnant and we were making an adoption plan. We had already met with a social worker, we were looking at profiles, and we would choose the parents.

That was it.

My parents were respectfully supportive. Heather's mom was incredible. Her father was not.

You're making a mistake. You're going to regret it. This is my grandson you're giving away.

He would stay in that position throughout the pregnancy and beyond. That sort of pressure was difficult. If we were teenagers, it would have had lasting repercussions—on

Heather, on us, on the child. But we were old enough to weather the resistance and work through it. And we had her mother. We had my parents and the adoption caseworker.

We had each other.

In a way, this crisis galvanized our relationship. I pushed through barriers that kept me from committing. The pregnancy was greater than the two of us, and we were both heading in the same direction, hand in hand, step for step.

We returned to school after the holidays, our decision intact. We pored through the profiles. There were certain attributes we were looking for, but mainly we wanted good people.

This was in the early days of adoption. Profiles were mainly handwritten letters and prospective parents didn't really know what to write. Nowadays, parenting hopefuls develop portfolios with video support. They develop a relationship with the birth mother, have regular meetings and attend doctor appointments. They even honor the occasion with a placement ceremony.

It was different back then.

The fear of an unstable birth mother kept some adoptive parents guarded. All it takes is one sensational story about a birth mother wanting her child back after placement and doors start locking.

Several profiles later, we weren't making a connection with any of the potential parents. Our hope began to wither. Abortion was still out, but if this adoption thing didn't work, there was only one decision left. That was still not a good one.

After asking for more profiles, we read about Wayne and Cathy. The next morning, we called the social worker.

FIVE

We met at the Italian Village Pizzeria.

It was a small family-owned restaurant with simple tables and wood paneling. There was a salad bar and an arcade in the back. We had something like it in the small town where we grew up. You went there for thin-sliced pizza and spaghetti and everyone knew everyone.

We met Wayne and Cathy at one of the vinyl booths.

Nervousness was the unwanted guest that joined us. We were excited, but terrified. If this didn't work out, then what? The clock was ticking. We weren't unreasonable but not willing to compromise. This had to work out.

No pressure.

Their five-year-old daughter, Kelsie, was with them. We loved that. They were unable to have a second child after her and that was why they were considering adoption. Kelsie was charming. I don't remember the conversation, but it was rather casual. Over breadsticks and spaghetti, our concerns were laid to rest.

We found our parents.

We told the social worker the next day. She started the

process. We still had many months to go, but at least we knew where we were going. The hard part was over. We had a destination.

Now to get there.

We finally told our friends what was happening. It wasn't a big announcement; we kept it relatively quiet. She hid the growing baby bump in baggy sweaters and sweatpants but still had to face occasional judgmental inquiries in our small town.

We kept our daily schedule, went to spring semester classes, and signed up for Lamaze. Childbirth was still quite a natural process at that point. This was before epidurals were vogue. There were drugs, but we were interested in avoiding them as much as possible. I say we, but she was doing most of the work.

I was a cheerleader.

The classes mostly taught us what was going to happen. There was a mucus plug. There was water that would break and one hundred percent effacement and ten centimeters of dilation. There was breech, the umbilical cord, a travel bag that needed to be packed. There would be pushing. But first, there would be breathing.

Breathing was our main defense.

We worked on a series of short breaths and cleansing breaths. I would coach her through the labor pain, help her focus, keep her present, feed her ice chips, rub her legs, her back, her arms, hands, neck, whatever she needed. She would be on the front line.

I was the medic.

We made it through spring semester without a hitch. Heather scored straight As. We stayed in on weekends and watched movies, kept a low profile and waited for things to happen. We were sort of excited.

This was going to work.

When the due date neared, we returned home. Heather's mother would fly back from Arizona for the birth. In the meantime, she stayed at her dad's house. I slept at my parents'. There were some difficulties with those arrangements, but we survived.

Michael arrived in June.

SIX

The contractions started. Then stopped. Then started.

We didn't know what to do.

The hospital was half an hour away. Despite Lamaze, our baby-making knowledge was mostly influenced by movies. We didn't want a baby delivered in the backseat so we got there super early. In fact, they were going to send us home. Then Heather's water broke.

They had to keep us.

I rubbed every part of her body for fifteen hours. She was shaking so badly that she needed a little something through the IV. Other than that, it was old-school pain management. We engaged the breathing practice, focused on something; she told me to get my breath out of her face. And that carefully packed travel bag lay in the corner.

It was a long night.

At some point, she was completely nude, covers on the floor and sweating on the sheets. People were coming and going, but no one cared because pain trumps modesty every single time.

It was close to 5:00 a.m.; Michael was on the way.

The doctor arrived in time to catch him. I stayed up top, my hot breath in her face, as they told her to push. The doctor inserted forceps, clamping Michael's tiny little head to pull him out.

It was about that time I was a sobbing mess.

Head on her shoulder, I wept uncontrollably. Maybe it was the stress or sleep deprivation, but full disclosure: I did the same thing with our following two kids. Complete and utter collapse.

Michael was a healthy boy.

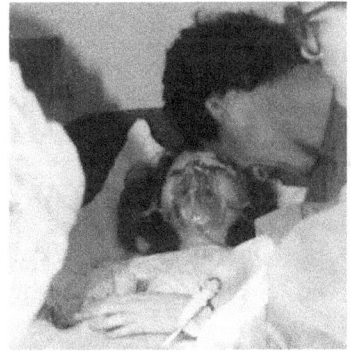

ILLINOIS LAW REQUIRED three days after birth before adoption papers could be signed. Heather and Michael stayed in the hospital all three days. Her sister and mother were there from Arizona. Her grandmother, too. She thought I was the greatest because she was from the old country and I was the man and that was all it took.

The birth certificate had to be filled out before we were

released. We called him Calvin Taylor Grant. His parents would name him Michael.

They got it right.

We made the decision to do the legal paperwork and placement outside the hospital. Steve had already signed adoption consent prior to the birth, in case he was the father. We drove Michael back to my parents' house. We were a couple of young adults with an infant in the backseat. Emotions were turbulent. We had prepared ourselves for this moment, but you can never really be ready for it. We had no doubts about our decision, but the gravity of what was happening was intensifying.

It was a long thirty-minute drive.

Our family and friends made it easier to do. In situations where there is no support, an adoption is extremely difficult. The birth mother bears the burden no matter what she does. She may doubt her decision whether she parents or places.

We were lucky.

My parents lived on a lake. The backyard was big and scenic. There was a picnic table beneath a sprawling hickory oak and a swing tied to a branch.

Wayne and Cathy met us there.

SEVEN

It was June.

The weather was fair and clear. Heather and I sat with a three-day-old infant. We held him and cuddled him but were not hesitant. We weren't ready to be parents, not when this crisis began and not now.

Wayne and Cathy met us beneath the oak tree.

We introduced them to their son and spent some time talking about the birth. They changed his diaper, and before long they were back on the road to make the long journey home. Nine months had passed. It had started with absolute crises and ended with a new family with a lot of hard work and stress in between. Our journey was over.

Just like that.

I THINK that's the hard part, for it to end so suddenly. How do you go through all of that and just return to life before it started? Despite our steady commitment, there was a period of emotional recovery that, at times, was difficult. But we never regretted it, not once, but it was sad for many reasons. And happy as well. We made it through an unplanned pregnancy. I finished college. Our relationship was as strong as ever. And Michael had an older sister and loving parents.

I returned to work at the research station.

In the fall, I started graduate school at the University of Illinois. Heather stayed in Carbondale to finish her undergraduate degree. We would travel on the weekends to stay at one place or the other. But before life resumed to normal, we would meet Wayne and Cathy one more time. It was at the hospital.

Blood was drawn.

It was an option, but paternity needed to be determined. If there were any health issues, it would be imperative to know the father's history. I gave a sample. Steve met us to provide a sample, too. And Michael, still an infant, had blood drawn from his foot. It took a few days for the results.

I was not the father.

At that point, I could say it didn't matter. To a large

degree, it didn't. What did it matter if I was his biological father or not? Michael had a family. But it was impossible not to feel some sadness.

Crisis is such.

The years passed and we kept in touch with Wayne and Cathy through letters. Cathy sent photos. Heather sent birthday cards. She finished college and moved in with me while she did an internship at a halfway house and I continued graduate school.

In 1992, we got married.

THE GREATEST FEAR of open adoption is the unknown.

It's the adoption tragedies that make the news, the disasters that get made into movies. In reality, open adoptions are often very cordial. For us, the correspondence helped us process the transition. Our top priority was always Michael. To see that happen, to witness his growth allowed us to grow with him from a distance. For adoptive parents, it helps to tell their child their adoption story and answer the inevitable questions many adoptees have about their birth parents.

The year we had married, we had mutually arranged to meet with Wayne and Cathy. They were going to move to Charleston, West Virginia. Michael was two years old.

We drove down to Southern Illinois and spent a few hours with them. We got to see him play, got to hold him. Got to say goodbye. That closure made all the difference. Two years after that, we would start our own family.

Ben was born.

When he crowned, I cried just as hard. Four years after that, there was Maddi, and despite my conviction that I'd been there, done that, I bawled a third time. Each time, Heather was exhausted and torn open and consoling me on her shoulder.

We were finally ready.

We did family things. We read books, we rolled on the floor, we went for walks and blew out birthday candles and sent them to school.

And every June, Heather would send a birthday card to Cathy.

As our kids were going to grade school, we watched Michael grow up. He knew about us and never had to second-guess why things were the way they were.

Eighteen years after giving birth, we would meet him again.

EIGHT

Heather had a bachelor's degree in administration of justice. Why AJ? Because that's what a lot of us do—go to college and get a degree and figure out the rest when the dust settles. So she took her degree in administration of justice and did the most logical thing.

She became a social worker.

It started out in drug and alcohol counseling at a halfway house in Champaign-Urbana. She was this young, attractive good girl helping people with hard-core addictions. Those were tough shoes to walk in. But she was resilient and loving and, as always, made her best efforts.

A few years later, she would work for Catholic Social Services.

This was the same agency that introduced us to open adoption. While her job titles varied, she would end up working as an adoption caseworker for the next twenty-five years.

Go figure.

She worked with adoptive parents, helping them

assemble portfolios, arranging meetings with potential birth mothers and handling the paperwork. Most importantly, she counselled them through waiting periods as well as the grieving process whenever an adoption didn't go as planned.

Her experiences varied greatly.

Sometimes she spent six or eight months with the birth mother, taking them to doctor's appointments, providing them with necessities, and counselling them through difficult emotions before and after delivery. Other times, she received a call from a hospital and arrived to meet the birth mother a day after delivery. Sometimes the adoption went well.

Other times, it did not.

She didn't always share her own experience. It all depended on whether it would be helpful or not. For birth mothers, it often was. Heather had been through the crises and survived. She knew the importance of counselling and support. She also realized how lucky she was to have had both.

Many birth mothers had neither.

Some were alone. Sometimes they lacked basic necessities or emotional coping skills, or had aggressive birth fathers that wanted them to keep the child, or aunts or grandparents or parents that weren't about to let them "give the baby away." One thing she always made clear.

Adoption was about love.

It wasn't getting rid of a problem or shucking responsibility. It was quite the opposite.

We made an adoption plan because we loved Michael. He needed a family that was ready for him, parents that were loving and stable and supportive. It's a risk, making an adoption plan. There's no guarantee the adoptive parents will be all those things. They're in the human struggle like the rest of us.

We were lucky.

Crises will make you grow up in a hurry. Our relationship had grown stronger. It wasn't perfect, they never are, but we had our footing. A foundation had been established beneath us. However, my dark years of depression were still upon me. It would be a few more years before I found my own way through counselling and meditation.

OUR CHILDREN WERE BORN in Illinois.

I was working on a golf course and Heather was still in adoption. I wanted to teach. The opportunity would arrive shortly after Maddi was born.

She was four months old when we moved to Charleston, South Carolina, where I began teaching horticulture at Trident Technical College. Heather stayed at home with the kids but resumed working as an adoption caseworker on a part-time basis. I was born in Charleston, Illinois, and thought it was coincidental that we would raise a family in Charleston, South Carolina. And Wayne and Cathy had moved to Charleston, West Virginia. That's a lot of Charlestons, but as coincidences go, it was nothing compared to when Michael came to visit.

This is where it gets weird.

To tell that story, I need to tell this one first. Several years ago, there was a news story about a family that had a safe word. I don't remember what the word was or even what it meant.

We just knew we wanted one.

So one night at dinner, we decided our secret word would be *hammer*. And hammer meant I love you. I don't remember if Heather was on board at first. Our kids have my sense of humor. We were sort of goofing on the whole secret-word thing. Not sort of. We were totally goofing on it.

But then it stuck.

We wrote little notes signed hammer, texts with hammer, waved goodbye saying hammer. It really became our weird secret word. In fact, it became a password for the longest time. Many of our accounts were assigned hammer88. The number had no significance. It was just something I tacked on when passwords required letters and numbers.

Hammer88.

In 2008, Heather received an email from Michael. He was eighteen years old. We had been receiving annual updates from Cathy and Wayne all this time. We saw him grow up, but now he was graduating high school.

And he wanted to visit.

Everything was in the room when the email arrived. Angst, elation, apprehension... it was all there. He was going on a road trip with two friends. We would meet them in Charleston. Times and dates and places were arranged, but that's not the odd part of this story. Sure, eighteen years separating us is not a common event. And why tell the whole story about secret words and hammers and passwords? Because it was Michael's email. His username.

Michaelhammer88.

Yeah. I know. You don't believe this. Neither do I. But it was there, I saw it. Heather saw it. His username contained our secret family word. Not only that, it had the number. *The number!*

THE WORD AND THE NUMBER.

How is this possible? It's not. It's just not.

But there we were looking at it. It was there. It happened. You might assume I'm spinning a yarn, adding spice to a story that's not really in need of it. The odds of that word and number are... *they're impossible.* We've shared our silly little inside secret word with very few people, but not our password and not with Cathy and Wayne. That's not something that went in a birthday card or was texted with directions.

This is nuts.

Sometimes I don't think I remember things correctly, like the time my grandma died. Heather and I were saying a prayer for her that night. We were still in college, kneeling down and reciting some Buddhist passage. When we were finished, my radio alarm turned on. There was no explanation for it, I didn't have the alarm set for nine o'clock at night. Maybe I just didn't look close enough, because alarms don't turn on randomly like that. There had to be an explanation I just wasn't seeing.

But hammer88 was there. That was real and we were looking at it; we couldn't explain it. Neither could Michael. He didn't really know why he used that word and number.

None of this felt real anymore.

This was some sort of surreal *Matrix* movie moment. I was waiting for the walls to melt. They didn't.

We met Michael in Charleston. The reunion was stunning. It's the stuff in movies. Charleston is an old Southern city, as charming as it is historical. There are horses pulling carriages and buildings that witnessed the Civil War. The harbor has a distinctive smell of pluff mud.

Nervously, we walked down the buckled sidewalks, holding hands like lost college kids. Our expectations were fluttering like kites without tails. Would he be happy to see us? Heather saw him from a block away.

They recognized each other.

They tearfully embraced on a broken street corner as tourists passed in horse-drawn carriages. They had no idea she'd waited eighteen years for this moment.

NINE

Looking back, crisis doesn't seem so bad.

In fact, our crisis turned out quite storybook. It would be easy to romanticize, to gloss over the bumps and bruises, the crying, the stress, the anguish and uncertainty—for us and those close to us, our families and friends. Michael.

Time, though, works its magic.

It smooths out the rough edges, takes the stink off a bad deal. They say forgetting is a blessing, a survival mechanism that eases our suffering. A brain wash that dulls the pain. Case in point, when Heather got a tattoo several years back, she insisted it hurt worse than childbirth. I was there for both of those events.

And begged to differ.

So why tell this story? I'm reminded of a cancer survivor who spoke about all the life lessons that were inherent in her struggle, the leaps and bounds of spiritual growth, how it renewed relationships and let the sun shine again. When asked if she was glad she got cancer, her response was curt.

Oh, hell no.

We were once invited to tell our story to a youth group.

It was a few years after Michael was born. By that time, the dust had settled and we were in a better place. Our presentation was upbeat and positive. Michael was a beautiful baby in a great family, and we unwittingly made it sound too easy, too wonderful.

Look what we did with an unplanned pregnancy; we made a beautiful flower, turned lemons into lemonade. And you can, too!

Some of the parents wanted to see more remorse and less *hey, no problem if you get pregnant, there's always adoption*. And I totally get that. We were lucky Cathy and Wayne were solid, lucky to have each other, lucky to have supportive parents. Maybe our message needed to be a little more real.

At least a little less rosy.

But we were happy. Happy for Michael, for Wayne and Cathy. Sometimes roses rise from ashes.

When we were older, we spoke with adoptive parents about our experience, in particular the open adoption aspect. Some parents are wary, and that makes total sense. Our experience provides a glimpse of what it can be, how healing can take place for everyone.

Adoption is sometimes referred to as the third option. That's last place. First is parenting and second is abortion. And then there's adoption. It's frightening. Scary as hell. Will there be regret? Will something go wrong? Will the birth mother change her mind, stalk us, get weird?

Unknowns, man.

So, yeah, I get that. Completely valid fears, all of them. Like I said, we had some luck fall our way.

So why tell this story? Because it's about what's possible. Because it wasn't until recently—twenty-six years after Michael's birth—that the entire journey felt complete. We weren't looking for it and didn't realize we'd reached it until after it happened. You'd think a sense of closure would've occurred with all the birthday and holiday correspondences, or when Michael sent the email with our secret password. Or when we reunited downtown.

It happened in New York City.

TEN

We received a wedding invitation in early 2016.

Michael was getting married in the spring. It would be in New York City, where he now lived. He grew up in Oklahoma and had spent most of his life there. Once he graduated high school, he moved to NYC.

The invitation was flattering. But of course, all sorts of thoughts followed. Is this just a kindly gesture? Would it be inappropriate to go? Or weird? He wouldn't have sent the invitation if he didn't want us to be there. Right? This went on for weeks.

Then we booked a flight.

Initially, I wasn't able to go. But, as luck would have it, plans unexpectedly changed. We flew out on a Saturday.

We'd never been to New York. It was intimidating, the unknown and all that. All we knew about New York was what we'd seen on television. In my experience, if your preparation involves movies, you're effed. We did some research which included stalking Michael's fiancé on Facebook. His name is Jeff.

Let me back up a step.

Michael is gay. Overall, it's a nonfactor, but it is relevant to the story. We knew that before we met him in Charleston. On that day we were struck by his calm demeanor. He knew exactly who he was. There didn't seem to be any conflict with his sexuality, with what he wanted in life and where he was going. It's something we all want and he seemed to have it.

We loved that.

So we stalked Jeff on Facebook. We weren't sending a friend request or anything, it was just the normal kind of stalking. The curious kind. What did he look like, was he a good kid, where did he come from? We drilled through photos and read his posts. There wasn't anything out of the ordinary, the usual social media memes and whatnot. We got what we wanted when I noticed a single line on his profile. It was in italics.

One mutual friend.

Remember the secret family password weirdness? Here it comes again.

Five minutes ago we didn't know Jeff and now we have a mutual friend? This wasn't Tom from MySpace. You don't have mutual friends unless you both know the same person. Facebook is a big world, so maybe it was something random.

It wasn't.

I know what you're thinking, but we're not linked with Michael on Facebook. We shouldn't have a mutual friend at all, and there it was. Our mutual friend was someone who had lived in New York City for the past twenty-six years. His name is Jamie.

And we went to high school with him.

Heather and I grew up in a small town tucked between

Illinois cornfields. It's a standard Midwestern town with clipped hedges and local taverns.

It's as far from New York City as it gets.

Heather and Jamie were good friends in middle school until he moved away. His career eventually took him to New York City in his mid-twenties and he'd lived there ever since. He moved to New York City twenty-six years ago. That was the year Michael was born. And Jamie knew Jeff.

Six degrees of Kevin Bacon can't touch this.

We arrived in New York before noon on Saturday and spent the afternoon with Jamie on the Lower East Side. It kept us occupied. We were very grateful he was there to settle our nerves. We were out of our element, in a new city, not sure what the evening would bring. Would they be happy to see us? Nervous? Is this weird?

Now we weren't so sure.

We asked someone at the hotel what was the best way to hail a cab. To the guy's credit, he didn't laugh in my face. Just raise your arm, he said. We arrived at the venue, early evening. The sun was hours from setting, the spring air cool and crisp. We walked a few blocks, taking in the sights, absorbing the city's energy.

Holding hands.

Had it really been twenty-six years? Is this really how the story ends—the crises that began tangled in sheets so long ago, when we were young and lost and scared, now just a distant memory? Will we wake up on the floor in the back of that college house and realize it was all just a dream? Because these things don't end this way.

There aren't happy endings like this.

We followed the crowd up an iron staircase, and for a moment, we were all alone. It was twenty-six years earlier, just a couple of nervous kids in a really big world, unsure which way to turn, what was around the corner. But in the next moment, we saw Cathy. There were tears. Hugs.

It was real again.

We caught up with Wayne and Cathy and a now grown-up and married Kelsie; we met extended family, recalled the day we met at the Italian Village. They were from the Midwest, so it didn't take long to speak the same language.

Had it really been twenty-six years?

THE CEREMONY TOOK place on a rooftop. Wayne and Cathy ushered Michael out. We sat in the crowd, unnoticed. Just another set of smiling faces. As dusk drew near, Michael and Jeff took their vows in a short ceremony among friends and family.

It would be another hour before we met Michael.

The reception took place downstairs. We found a table in the corner. It was small and convenient, one where we could stand up and hold our drinks.

An inconspicuous place.

It wasn't until later that we realized it was perfect. The family graciously invited us to the table, but we declined. From our little corner, we watched an extravagant New York City crowd mix with Midwesterners—a clash of styles and values, interests and eras. But a crowd united in love.

Michael and Jeff had great families.

Our reunion was what you would imagine. As tears spilled and knees buckled, I was waiting for walls to melt, to realize I had fallen sleep. I was just a character who had forgotten this was a movie. Perched in our corner, we watched the night unfold. We were not removed, not distant or antisocial. We spent time with all the family and friends.

The fathers gave touching speeches about their sons. And when the cake was cut and, one by one, friends toasted the newlyweds, Heather and I made our exit. We thanked them for being the family anyone would wish for. They had exceeded all our hopes. The script of this moment was surreal.

And perfect.

The night was relatively young, but we'd done everything we'd come to do in New York City. We ate a slice of pizza in a very small hotel room and fell asleep.

ELEVEN

So why tell this story?

The world needs to hear it is a tad presumptuous of me to think. The world doesn't need to hear it. And this certainly isn't the end of anything. But for some reason, it certainly feels like it. Twenty-six years ago, we would not have been so bold as to write a storybook tale like this, and certainly not this ending.

But I like a good ending. And this certainly felt worthy.

Even if it is true.

EPILOGUE

Heather, Michael, and Cathy

ABOUT THE AUTHOR

Tony Bertauski is a horticulture instructor by day and a writer at times in between. He and Heather still live in Charleston with their two dogs, Jake and Aussie.

Their kids, Ben and Maddi, aren't kids anymore.

bertauski.com

www.ingramcontent.com/pod-product-compliance
Lightning Source LLC
Chambersburg PA
CBHW052107110526
44591CB00013B/2384